BASKETBALL'S ORIGIN STORY

by Matt Chandler

CAPSTONE PRESS
a capstone imprint

Published by Capstone Press, an imprint of Capstone
1710 Roe Crest Drive, North Mankato, Minnesota 56003
capstonepub.com

Copyright © 2025 by Capstone. All rights reserved. No part of this publication may be reproduced in whole or in part, or stored in a retrieval system, or transmitted in any form or by any means, electronic, mechanical, photocopying, recording, or otherwise, without written permission of the publisher.

SPORTS ILLUSTRATED KIDS is a trademark of ABG-SI LLC.
Used with permission.

Library of Congress Cataloging-in-Publication Data
Names: Chandler, Matt, author.
Title: Basketball's origin story / by Matt Chandler.
Description: North Mankato, Minnesota : Capstone Press, 2025. | Series: Sports illustrated kids: sports origin stories | Includes bibliographical references and index. | Audience: Ages 8-11 | Audience: Grades 4-6 | Summary: "A scramble for the rebound! A three-point shot at the buzzer! You love the excitement of basketball. But where and how did this hoop-sinking sport begin? What were the original rules? What equipment did players use? And how has the sport changed since then? Get the answers to all your questions and more!" — Provided by publisher.
Identifiers: LCCN 2024022731 (print) | LCCN 2024022732 (ebook) | ISBN 9781669090328 (hardcover) | ISBN 9781669090274 (paperback) | ISBN 9781669090281 (pdf) | ISBN 9781669090304 (kindle edition) | ISBN 9781669090298 (epub)
Subjects: LCSH: Basketball—History—Juvenile literature.
Classification: LCC GV885.1 .C42 2025 (print) | LCC GV885.1 (ebook) | DDC 796.323—dc23/eng/20240520
LC record available at https://lccn.loc.gov/2024022731
LC ebook record available at https://lccn.loc.gov/2024022732

Editorial Credits
Editor: Mandy Robbins; Designer: Elyse White; Media Researcher: Jo Miller; Production Specialist: Tori Abraham

Image Credits
Alamy: Heritage Image Partnership Ltd, 19, Witold Skrypczak, 8, Alpha Stock , 17, GL Archive, 6, Hum Images, 18, Imago History Collection, 7, RBM Vintage Images, 14; AP Images: Ed Maloney, File, 20, Jessica Hill, File, 12, 27, Jack Dempsey, Pool, 4; Erie Times-News via AP/Christopher Millette, 25; Getty Images: FatCamera, 28, Library of Congress, 9, Markus Boesch, 15; Las Vegas Sun via AP: Steve Marcus, 24; Shutterstock: JoffreyM, cover (top); Sports Illustrated: Erick W. Rasco, 10, John W. McDonough, 22, 26, Manny Millan, 21; Wikimedia: Northwest Digital Heritage/Whitman County Library, cover (bottom), public domain, 11

Quotes Source:
p. 5, 9: *James Naismith's Life and Legacy: Celebrating 150 Years.* University of Kansas.
https://exhibits.lib.ku.edu/exhibits/show/naismith150/collections/radio-interview, Accessed June 11, 2024.

Any additional websites and resources referenced in this book are not maintained, authorized, or sponsored by Capstone. All product and company names are trademarks™ or registered® trademarks of their respective holders.

Printed and bound in China. 6090

TABLE OF CONTENTS

INTRODUCTION
DENVER TURNS DOWN THE HEAT............4

CHAPTER 1
MEET JAMES NAISMITH...................6

CHAPTER 2
PEACH BASKETS AND SOCCER BALLS......10

CHAPTER 3
THE EARLY GAME OF BASKETBALL.........16

CHAPTER 4
A NEW ERA............................20

CHAPTER 5
TODAY'S GAME........................24

Timeline................................29
Glossary...............................30
Read More..............................31
Internet Sites.........................31
Index..................................32
About the Author.......................32

Words in **bold** are in the glossary.

INTRODUCTION
DENVER TURNS DOWN THE HEAT

The 2022–23 Denver Nuggets finished the regular season with the best record in the National Basketball Association's (NBA) Western Conference. Led by superstar center Nikola Jokić, the Nuggets made it to the NBA Finals against the Miami Heat.

The Nuggets' Bruce Brown takes a shot against the Miami defense.

Denver took a 3–1 series lead. They were one win away from the NBA Championship! Game 5 was epic. The Heat, led by Bam Adebayo and Jimmy Butler, were fighting to keep their season alive. With under two minutes to play, the Heat took the lead 89–88. Just when it looked like the Heat might force a Game 6, Nuggets guard Bruce Brown snatched a **rebound**. He banked in a shot with 1 minute, 31 seconds left in the game. It was enough! The defense shut down the Heat. The Nuggets were NBA champs!

Basketball is packed with thrilling moments. Would you believe all this excitement can be traced back to bored college students and a creative teacher?

Nuggets center Nikola Jokić scored 600 points in the playoffs and was named Most Valuable Player (MVP) of the Finals.

CHAPTER 1
MEET JAMES NAISMITH

In 1891, Massachusetts was hit by a huge snowstorm. If not for the storm, the game of basketball might have never been invented!

Dr. James Naismith was a gym teacher there at Springfield College. During the storm, his students couldn't go outside to play football. Stuck inside, the students quickly grew bored. That is when Naismith had an idea.

James Naismith

Naismith (center in suit) poses with the very first basketball team.

"I called the boys to the gym, divided them up into teams of nine, and gave them an old soccer ball," Naismith said in a 1939 radio interview. "I showed them two peach baskets I'd nailed up at each end of the gym. I told them the idea was to throw the ball into the opposing team's peach basket." The game of basketball was born.

Though his students loved it, Naismith's game did not have enough rules. Players were tackling each other on the court like they did in football games. Fights broke out.

In 1892, Naismith developed the original 13 rules of basketball. His rules set time limits, **fouls**, and explained the correct way to handle the ball. Naismith said the most important rule for player safety was rule number three—a player cannot run holding the ball.

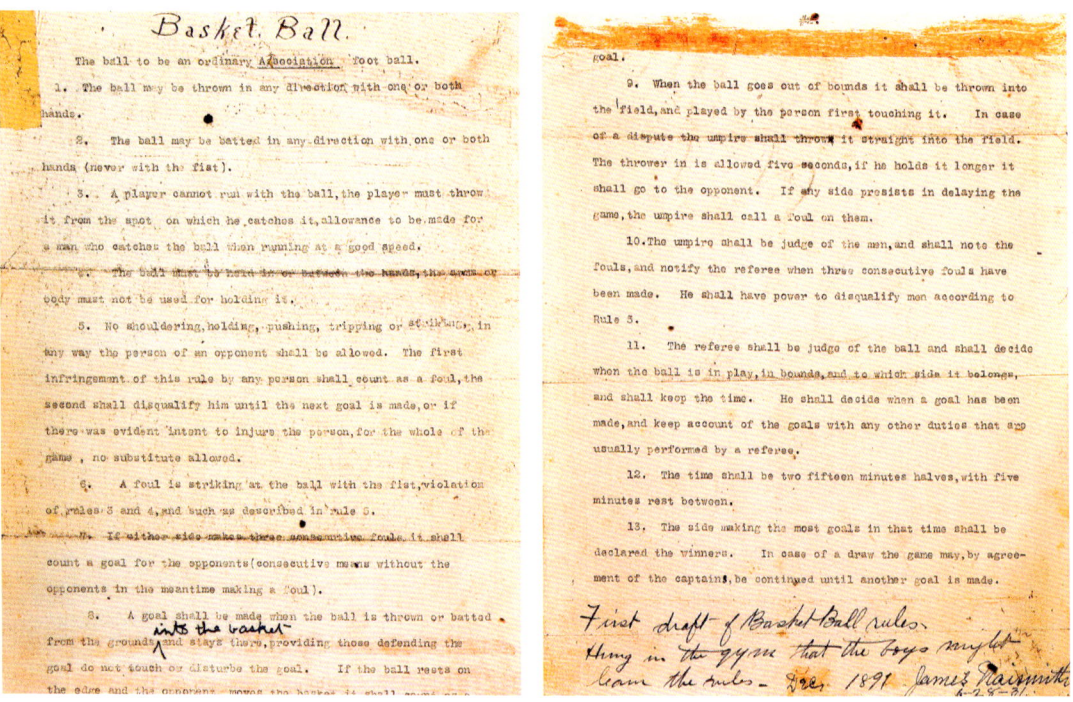

Naismith's original rules of basketball

An 1899 high school basketball game in Washington, D.C.

"We tried out the game with those rules and we didn't have one **casualty**," he said. "We had a fine, clean sport."

Naismith sent the new rules to athletic clubs across the country. Within 10 years, basketball was a national sport. The game that began with two peach baskets and a soccer ball was a huge success!

In 2010, Naismith's original typed copy of his rules for basketball sold at auction for $3.8 million!

CHAPTER 2
PEACH BASKETS AND SOCCER BALLS

Today, Steph Curry can advance the ball up the court and score in seconds. The speed of the game makes basketball exciting. In 1891, things were different. Each time a player scored, someone had to climb a ladder to get the ball out of the peach basket. Soon, the bottoms were removed from the baskets, allowing the ball to fall through after a shot. This began the **evolution** of the sport.

Steph Curry advances the ball.

Naismith decided to create a unique ball for playing basketball. The original ball was made of leather and laced together like a football. It was 4 inches (10.2 centimeters) larger than a standard soccer ball. By 1949, the laces were gone. Today's ball measures 29.5 inches (75 cm) for men and 28.5 inches (72.4 cm) for women.

Antique basketball

BASKETBALL AROUND THE GLOBE

The NBA may be the most famous professional league, but basketball is a global game. Teams from 22 different countries have won Olympic medals in basketball.

The EuroLeague boasts 18 teams. NBA star Luka Dončić began his career there. The Turkish Basketball Super League and the Chinese Basketball Association are among many leagues worldwide producing basketball superstars.

Women's leagues in Turkey, Spain, and Russia also showcase **elite** players from around the world. But the highest level of female play is the Women's National Basketball Association (WNBA).

11

RIMS AND BACKBOARDS

Hearing a three-pointer from WNBA star Sabrina Ionescu whistling through the net is an exciting sound. Today's nets and metal rims are a long way from Naismith's peach baskets.

Sabrina Ionescu takes a shot from the three-point line.

Just four years after the first game was played, a metal basketball rim was used. The rim was made of iron and had an 18-inch (46-cm) **diameter**. It was mounted on a wooden backboard. Iron rims were soon replaced by wire.

The traditional glass backboard was invented in the 1940s. The glass backboard allowed the players to see rebounds better.

In the 1970s, breakaway rims were added. These rims were designed to have flexibility. They bent when pulled or hung on. It allowed players like Atlanta Hawks big man Dominique Wilkins to dominate opponents with his famous windmill dunk.

Salaries for NBA players when the league was formed averaged $4,000 to $5,000 per season. In 2024, Steph Curry of the Golden State Warriors earned $51.9 million!

UNIFORMS AND SHOES

In the early years of basketball, there were no uniforms. Women were required to wear long wool skirts. Men often wore pants and a sweater. Can you imagine LeBron James playing 40 minutes a night in a sweater?

By 1901, basketball shorts and sleeveless shirts were introduced for men. As the game became more popular, team names and logos were added to the jerseys. Women had to play in skirts until the 1960s.

A 1905 women's basketball team

In 1917, Converse created the first basketball shoe, the Converse All-Star. It was the highest-selling basketball shoe for decades. By the 1980s, Reebok, Nike, Adidas, Converse, and Puma were all competing to create the safest, best-performing basketball shoes.

Converse All-Star shoes, 1992

Today, many NBA superstars have their own shoe design. These shoes generate billions of dollars in sales to people who don't even play basketball!

FACT

In the 1950s, an inventor designed a shoe with suction cups on the bottom to help players stop more quickly. The idea was based on the tentacles of an octopus!

CHAPTER 3
THE EARLY GAME OF BASKETBALL

The first professional basketball league was created in 1898. The National Basketball League (NBL) was formed in Philadelphia, Pennsylvania. Horace Fogel, a newspaper editor, is credited with organizing the six-team league.

On December 1, 1898, the first professional game was played. The Trenton Nationals defeated the Hancock Athletic Association. By 1903, two other professional leagues formed.

Horace Fogel

The New England League and the Massachusetts Central League were new and needed players. To build up these leagues, a group of businessmen traveled from Massachusetts to Philadelphia in the summer of 1903. They **recruited** the best players from the NBL to join the new leagues. Without its star players, the NBL could not finish the 1903–04 schedule. The league was shut down.

COLLEGE BALLERS

On February 7, 1893, Vanderbilt University in Nashville, Tennessee, became the first college in America to play an organized basketball game. The men's squad challenged the local YMCA squad.

On April 4, 1896, two women's college teams made history. Stanford University took on the University of California in the first women's basketball game between college teams. Stanford broke a 1–1 tie with a game-winning shot by Agnes Morley! Stanford won the game 2–1.

Georgetown Prep basketball team, early 1900s

Students at William Street Girls School play basketball on the playground in 1908.

Over the next decade, basketball squads formed at colleges and universities across America and around the world. This would lead to the expansion of professional leagues, as those players looked to continue playing after graduation.

FACT

Men were banned from the first women's college basketball game. Even the media could only send women to cover the historic game. Inside the gym, a crowd of 700 women cheered on the two squads.

CHAPTER 4
A NEW ERA

In 1946, the Basketball Association of America (BAA) was founded. Within three years, the league merged with the NBL, which had been relaunched in 1937. The new league became known as the National Basketball Association (NBA).

George Mikan was the first NBA star. The 6-foot, 10-inch (208-cm) center led the Minneapolis Lakers to seven championships.

George Mikan takes a shot in a 1949 game.

Magic Johnson takes a shot in a 1980 game.

By the 1950s, fans began to lose interest. More than half of the teams shut down. The league knew it had to make the game more exciting to watch. They did, and the fans began to come back.

In the 1960s and 1970s, the NBA expanded. By 1980, superstars Larry Bird and Magic Johnson had created a new level of excitement. Soon Michael Jordan would join the league. The league that almost shut down in the early 1950s proved it was here to stay!

CHANGING THE RULES

There have been many changes since Naismith published the original 13 rules of basketball. Early on, a new rule awarded a free throw for any player who was fouled. In 1954, the NBA added the **24-second clock** to speed up the game and increase scoring.

The 24-second clock is often called the shot clock.

Today, watching superstars like Caitlin Clark drain threes is one of the most exciting parts of a game. In 1967, the American Basketball Association (ABA) added a three-point shot. That same year, it led to one of the most exciting finishes to a game. The Indiana Pacers trailed the Dallas Chaparrals 118–116 with one second left on the clock. Jerry Harness took the inbound pass and launched a 92-foot (28-meter) shot. The shot banked off the backboard and went in! The Pacers pulled off a miracle win!

THE WNBA

Elena Delle Donne. Sue Bird. Aliyah Boston. Breanna Stewart. Before 1996, these talented players would have finished college and had no options to play professionally in the United States. Then the NBA launched the Women's National Basketball Association (WNBA). What began as an eight-team league has grown to 12 teams packed with superstars. Today, the WNBA has a loyal fan base. Players earn more money than ever before. Attendance is rising. More games are being televised. Most importantly, future female basketball players no longer must see their playing days end when they graduate from college.

CHAPTER 5
TODAY'S GAME

From youth teams to college to the pros, basketball has global appeal. The NBA earns $3.3 billion from television alone! It is the most watched American sports league worldwide.

WNBA television ratings have increased as well, and more fans are attending the games. In 2023, the Las Vegas Aces set a record when 17,406 fans attended their game against the Phoenix Mercury.

Las Vegas Aces guard Chelsea Gray takes a shot against the Phoenix Mercury.

Internationally, basketball is thriving. The EuroLeague sells out arenas as the best players from Russia, Spain, Turkey, and beyond compete. Europe has also produced NBA superstars such as Luka Dončić and Giannis Antetokounmpo.

NATIONAL WHEELCHAIR BASKETBALL ASSOCIATION

Thanks to the National Wheelchair Basketball Association (NWBA), athletes who use a wheelchair can play basketball at a high level. Wheelchair basketball began in the 1940s. Many soldiers returning from World War II (1939–1945) needed wheelchairs. Since then, the NWBA has grown to include more than 200 teams from around the world.

2016 NWBA championship tournament game

FROM PLAYGROUNDS TO SUPERSTARS

Many kids who play basketball dream of making it to the pros. Check out a few of the biggest superstars who made their dreams come true.

Giannis Antetokounmpo was a first-round draft pick of the Milwaukee Bucks in 2013. He led the Bucks to the title in 2021. He is a two-time league Most Valuable Player (MVP) and eight-time All-Star.

Giannis Antetokounmpo takes the ball down the court for the Milwaukee Bucks.

Breanna Stewart takes a shot for the Seattle Storm.

Breanna Stewart was named **Rookie** of the Year with the Seattle Storm in 2016. She has earned five trips to the All-Star Game. Stewart is considered one of her generation's greatest **clutch** shooters.

Patrick Anderson has been a force in wheelchair basketball for more than 20 years. He led Canada to back-to-back World Championships in 1997 and 2001. Anderson also led Canada to gold medals at the 2000 and 2004 Paralympic Games.

It is estimated that more than 450 million people play organized basketball. It is a game that almost anyone can play anywhere in the world. Virtually every city has basketball courts that are free to use. With a single ball, a large group of players can enjoy the game.

The game of basketball has speed, excitement, high-scoring games, and accessibility. It's no wonder it is one of the most popular sports in the world!

TIMELINE

1891 James Naismith invents the game of basketball.

1896 The first women's college game is played between Stanford University and the University of California at Berkeley.

1898 The first professional basketball league, the National Basketball League (NBL), is formed.

1936 Basketball is added as a medal event at the Olympic Games.

1949 The National Basketball Association (NBA) is formed.

1950 Professional basketball is **integrated**.

1966 The Boston Celtics win a record eighth consecutive NBA Championship in a row.

1996 The Women's National Basketball Association (WNBA) is formed.

1999 Wang Zhizhi becomes the first Asian-born player ever drafted to play in the NBA.

2022 LeBron James becomes the first active player in basketball history to have a net worth of $1 billion.

GLOSSARY

24-second clock (TWEN-tee-for SEK-und CLOK)—a clock that counts down once a team has gained control of the ball; they have 24 seconds to take a shot

casualty (KAZH-uhl-tee)—when a person is hurt or injured

clutch (KLUHCH)—describes a player who does well under pressure

diameter (dye-AM-uh-tur)—the length of a straight line through the center of a circle

elite (i-LEET)—among the best

evolution (ev-uh-LOO-shuhn)—when something develops over time with gradual changes

foul (FOUL)—an action that is against the rules

integrate (IN-tuh-grayt)—to include people of all races

rebound (REE-bound)—to take possession of the ball after it bounces off the backboard or rim

recruit (ri-KROOT)—to ask someone to join a team

rookie (RUH-kee)—a first-year player

salary (SAL-uh-ree)—the amount of money a person makes in a year

READ MORE

Berglund, Bruce. *Basketball GOATS: The Greatest Athletes of All Time*. North Mankato, MN: Capstone, 2022.

Chandler, Matt. *Basketball's Best Coaches: Influencers, Leaders, and Winners on the Court*. North Mankato, MN: Capstone, 2024.

Moore, Madison. *More Than Just a Game: The Black Origins of Basketball*. Chicago: Albert Whitman & Company, 2021.

INTERNET SITES

Basketball Hall of Fame
hoophall.com

EuroBasket
eurobasket.com

Women's National Basketball Association
wnba.com

INDEX

24-second clock, 22

Adebayo, Bam, 5
American Basketball Association (ABA), 23
Anderson, Patrick, 27
Antetokounmpo, Giannis, 25, 26

Basketball Association of America (BAA), 20
Bird, Larry, 21
Brown, Bruce, 4, 5

Clark, Caitlin, 23
college basketball, 18–19, 29
Curry, Steph, 10, 13

Dončić, Luka, 11, 25

EuroLeague, 11, 25

Fogel, Horace, 16, 17

Ionescu, Sabrina, 12

James, LeBron, 14, 29
Johnson, Magic, 21
Jokić, Nikola, 4, 5
Jordan, Michael, 21

Naismith, Dr. James, 6–9, 11, 12, 22, 29
National Basketball Association (NBA), 4, 5, 11, 13, 15, 20, 21, 22, 23, 24, 25, 29
National Basketball League (NBL), 16, 17, 20, 29
National Wheelchair Basketball Association (NWBA), 25, 27

Olympic Games, 11, 29

Paralympic Games, 27

rules, 8–9, 22, 23

shoes, 15
Stewart, Breanna, 23, 27

three-point shots, 12, 23

uniforms, 14

Wilkins, Dominique, 13
Women's National Basketball Association (WNBA), 11, 12, 23, 24, 29

ABOUT THE AUTHOR

Matt Chandler is the author of more than 85 books for children, including *Side-by-Side Baseball Stars*, which won the 2015 Outstanding Children's Book Award from the American Society of Journalists and Authors. Matt lives in New York with his wife, Amber, and his children, Zoey and Oliver. www.mattchandlerwriting.com